A Night in the Theatre

by

Lawrence Casler

SAMUEL FRENCH, INC.

45 WEST 25TH STREET   NEW YORK 10010

7623 SUNSET BOULEVARD HOLLYWOOD 90046

LONDON   TORONTO

Copyright © 1993, 1999 by Lawrence Casler

To Erika

IMPORTANT BILLING AND CREDIT REQUIREMENTS

All producers of A NIGHT IN THE THEATRE *must* give credit to the Author of the Play in all programs distributed in connection with performances of the Play and in all instances in which the title of the Play appears for purposes of advertising, publicizing or otherwise exploiting the Play and/or a production. The name of the Author *must* also appear on a separate line, on which no other name appears, immediately following the title, and *must* appear in size of type not less than fifty percent the size of the title type.

AUTHOR'S NOTES

• Characters

There are four characters with speaking roles: Margaret, Stanley, Donna, and Walter. All are in their mid-30s.

• Costumes

Both women are to be dressed appropriately for attending a play. Donna wears jewelry that jangles noisily.

Walter is conservatively dressed. Stanley wears a garish, tasteless sports jacket and non-matching tie.

• Alternatives for Staging

There are at least three ways of staging the play, all of which involve very simple settings. The choice depends partly on the physical set-up of the theater, but mostly on the preferences of the director.

1. (The most daring.) The four characters are never seen. Their voices are heard (body microphones probably necessary) as if they are members of the audience. On stage, Shakespeare's *Hamlet* is mimed. If this alternative is selected, separate performers will be needed for Hamlet, Claudius, Gertrude, Ghost, Ophelia, Horatio, Laertes, Polonius, Rosenkrantz and Guildenstern, Osric, Grave Diggers, Fortinbras, Priest, and Soldiers

(doubling is okay). For this alternative, Stanley and Walter should have voices distinctively different from one another, as should Margaret and Donna. If this first alternative is selected, the four characters can be seen taking their seats. When the theater is darkened, they will be invisible until the lights are up.

2. The four characters are seated on stage, side by side, with their backs to the audience. Seats should resemble theater seats.

3. The four characters are seated on stage, side by side, facing the audience. Seats should resemble theater seats.

A NIGHT IN THE THEATRE

ACT I

(Enter MARGARET, DONNA, WALTER, and STANLEY.)

WALTER. This is it. I think this is it. It must be these four seats. Go ahead, Margaret. You go first.

MARGARET. Where are the seat numbers? I hate it when they put the seat numbers where you can't see them.

WALTER. This must be it. This is where the usher pointed.

MARGARET. You can't trust ushers. I used to be an usher, and I never knew what I was doing. I just put people wherever there were empty seats.

WALTER. Just sit down, Margaret. Don't worry.

MARGARET. I thought we would be more in the center. This is sort of to the side. Why are we so far back? Will we be able to hear anything?

WALTER. Stanley, do you want to sit next to your wife?

STANLEY. Nah. Let the two girls sit together.

DONNA. Don't call us girls. I hate it when you do that.

(All four sit, side by side.)

MARGARET. We have to change places. I want to be next to the aisle.

WALTER. Why?

STANLEY. Don't you remember? She's always afraid of a fire. In case of a fire, she wants to get out in a hurry.

WALTER. What about us, Margaret? The rest of us want to get out, too.

MARGARET. But you're not as afraid as I am. Please.

(ALL stand up, clumsily and noisily shift positions, and sit. MARGARET is now at one end of the group; DONNA is at the other.)

MARGARET. Thank you.

DONNA. We have to change seats. I want to sit next to you, Margaret. We haven't talked together for ages.

WALTER. Are you kidding? We were all in the restaurant together half an hour ago.

DONNA. I mean really talked.

(ALL stand up, clumsily and noisily shift positions, and sit.)

WALTER. Are we finally ready? Can they start the play?

DONNA. Don't be sarcastic.

(Pause.)

MARGARET. Can everybody see?

STANLEY. There's nothing to see. It hasn't begun yet.

MARGARET. If we can't see, we can move closer. I see some empty seats way up toward the front. If they stay empty, we can move to the front. They don't care if you do that. In fact, I read somewhere that the actors and actresses like it when they can see people up front. They put on a better performance. That's why the acting is so bad on TV. There isn't a live audience.

DONNA. I don't like to be too close. When you're that close, you can see them spit. I hate it when they spit. It spoils the illusion. In the movies, you never see them spit. Even in close-ups, they never spit. Why is that?

MARGARET. I don't know. Walter, why is that?

WALTER. Why is what?

MARGARET. Why don't the actors and actresses ever spit in the movies?

STANLEY. Why don't you ask me? Why do you always ask Walter?

WALTER. They do spit. But in the movies it can be cut out. It can be edited. When they spit, it's called a gaff. The person who cuts it out is called a gaffer.

MARGARET. *(To Donna.)* You're lucky to have Walter. Stanley doesn't know anything about anything.

DONNA. You hear that, Walter? Margaret says I'm lucky I have you.

WALTER. She's right.

MARGARET. What did you want to ask me? Donna? What did you want to ask me?

STANLEY. Do they have a bar here? I want to get a drink before the show starts.

WALTER. You don't have time. It's curtain time right now.

STANLEY. These things never begin on time. We have at least five minutes yet. You want a drink?

WALTER. Quiet. The lights are going out. It's beginning.

STANLEY. Damn it. Why do they always have to begin these things on time?

(If the first staging alternative is selected, the stage is now slightly lit. The miming of Shakespeare's play now begins. It continues through the characters' conversations and through the parenthetical pauses.)

MARGARET. Has it begun? It's so dark. Why is it so dark?

WALTER. It's supposed to be midnight. So it's dark.

MARGARET. Can you see? What are they doing?

WALTER. Listen.

(Pause.)

MARGARET. Can you see, Donna?

DONNA. Yes. These seats aren't too bad. Can *you* see?

MARGARET. Barely. I can see barely. Stanley, can you see?

STANLEY. Sure I can see.

MARGARET. Can you see, Walter?
WALTER. I can see. I can see.

(Pause.)

DONNA. Who's that?
STANLEY. That's Hamlet.
WALTER. That's not Hamlet. That's the ghost.
STANLEY. Walter says that's the ghost.
MARGARET. He doesn't look like a ghost. He's not realistic.
WALTER. Ghosts can't be realistic. They aren't real.
STANLEY. Where's his white sheet?
WALTER. Ghosts don't have to have sheets.
MARGARET. Did I tell you what Jason wants to dress up as for Halloween?
DONNA. No. What?
WALTER. Will the two of you kindly shut up? I came here to listen to Shakespeare, not your yackety-yacking.
MARGARET. Look who's yackety-yacking. He's going to dress up like Elvis Presley. Isn't that original?

(Stage DARKENS.)

STANLEY. Look, it got dark. The first act is over already. That was fast. Who ever said Shakespeare is slow?
DONNA. *(Standing up.)* It's intermission already? Good. I'll go to the ladies' room. Did you notice where the ladies' room is?

WALTER. It's not intermission. They're just changing the scene. You can't go to the bathroom when they're just changing the scene.

DONNA. *(Sits down.)* Okay. I can hold in.

WALTER. So hold in.

DONNA.. It isn't good to hold in. It isn't good for your bladder. I saw on one of my shows there was this woman who held in, and her bladder exploded. She lives in North Dakota or one of those places.

WALTER. Don't believe everything you see on TV. They could be faking. There are young actors and actresses, they're called fledgling actors and actresses, who get paid for saying their bladders exploded.

DONNA. That's ridiculous. If it's on TV, it has to be true. The FCC makes sure it's true.

STANLEY. You're showing your ignorance. It's the FAA.

WALTER. *You're* showing *your* ignorance. The FAA has nothing to do with television. It's the Federal Agriculture Administration. They make sure farmers don't inject cancer germs into their chickens.

MARGARET. I never knew that. You know everything. Donna, I still think you should go if you want to. Do you want to go?

DONNA. I don't have to go any more. Talking about it made the urge go away.

STANLEY. That's how Margaret is about sex. If you talk about it, the urge goes away.

DONNA. Hush. Who's that?

STANLEY. I think that's Hamlet. Is that Hamlet?

WALTER. No, that's the king. That's Hamlet's uncle.

(Pause.)

MARGARET. My throat is dry.

(Loud RUSTLING of cellophane.)

DONNA. Is that a mint? My throat is dry, too.

MARGARET. You want a mint?

DONNA. You have a mint? What flavor?

MARGARET. I think it's peppermint. You want peppermint?

DONNA. Do you have cinnamon? I like cinnamon.

MARGARET. No. I think it's peppermint. It's so dark in here I can't tell. You want one?

DONNA. Yes, I'll have a mint. Thank you.

(Loud RUSTLING of cellophane.)

WALTER. Will you please cut out the racket?

DONNA. I just want a mint. My throat is dry.

WALTER. Whenever we're someplace where you're supposed to be quiet, your throat gets dry. You're the original dry throat.

MARGARET. Stanley? Walter? You want a mint? (*No answer.*) Stanley? Walter? Who said "shhh"? Did you say "shhh"?

WALTER. The person in front of you said "shhh." Will you pipe down and watch the play? This is a good part that's coming.

DONNA. What's happening? What are they talking about?

WALTER. Just listen.

DONNA. I'm listening, but they talk funny. Why don't they modernize their talking so people can understand? It's like a foreign language they're talking. Isn't it like a foreign language they're talking, Margaret?

MARGARET. I don't know. I haven't been listening. I'm waiting for something to happen.

WALTER. Something *is* happening. This guy wants to go back to school, and the king says it's okay with him if it's okay with his father, and his father says it's okay.

MARGARET. Did you hear that, Donna? That fellow wants to go to school.

DONNA. That's nice. Who? Which one wants to go to school?

MARGARET. I think that one. The scrawny one. Stanley, which one wants to go to school? (*Pause.*) Stanley? Wake up, Stanley. You do this every time we go anywhere. You embarrass me.

STANLEY. I wasn't sleeping. I was resting my eyes. I can tell you everything that has happened. There's this ghost, and there's this king, and it all happens in Denmark.

MARGARET. I don't blame you for sleeping. This is Shakespeare? This is supposed to be interesting? Why is that one in black talking so much?

WALTER. Quiet. That's Hamlet. He's thinking out loud. He's sad because his father died and because his mother got married so soon.

MARGARET. I'd be sad, too. You know whose father died last week? Jack's father.

STANLEY. Jack died?

DONNA. Who's Jack?

MARGARET. *Jack*. You remember Jack.

STANLEY. Jack died? Did you say Jack died? He was a young man.

MARGARET. Not Jack. Jack's father. He was in his sixties. His mid-sixties.

STANLEY. That's young. Mid-sixties is young.

MARGARET. He was maybe sixty-five, sixty-six.

STANLEY. Sixty-five, sixty-six, that's young. The older I get, the younger I think mid-sixties is.

DONNA. Why are they playing those trumpets? I thought you said this wasn't a musical. I don't know what's happening.

WALTER. If you paid attention you would know. Pay attention. The king — you see him, with the crown? — just said that when he dies, Hamlet will be king. You see that woman? That's Gertrude. His mother. Hamlet's mother.

DONNA. Of course that's his mother. You didn't have to tell me that. What's she trying to do? Cheer him up?

WALTER. Yes, cheer him up.

STANLEY. Everybody's leaving the stage. Is it intermission? No, that one is staying.

WALTER. That's Hamlet who's staying. Listen.

(Loud JANGLING from Donna's jewelry.)

WALTER. Donna, please! You're disturbing me. You're disturbing everyone in the theater. Why do you take noisy jewelry to the theater?

DONNA. It goes with my outfit. Why did you buy it for me if you didn't want me to wear it?

STANLEY. Why is that guy talking to nobody?

WALTER. This is what is called a soliloquy.

STANLEY. No, it isn't. You think you know everything. The soliloquy is when he says "to be or not to be." This is something else.

WALTER. This is another soliloquy. Whenever you talk to yourself, it's called a soliloquy.

MARGARET. When Jack's father talked to himself they didn't call it a soliloquy. They called it Alzheimers.

STANLEY. Who has Alzheimers?

MARGARET. Had. Jack's father.

DONNA. Enough about Jack's father. It's too depressing. Who just came on stage? Those men just walked on stage.

WALTER. Some soldiers. And Horatio. He's a friend of Hamlet.

STANLEY. Horatio. Where do they get names like that? Is that a Danish name?

WALTER. Yes. Horatio is a Danish name.

STANLEY. And Gertrude? The mother? You're going to tell me that's a Danish name? That's not a Danish name.

WALTER. Gertrude is Danish. It was originally Danish.

MARGARET. That reminds me. I'm getting hungry.

DONNA. They're saying they saw the ghost, right?

WALTER. Congratulations. That's right.

STANLEY. The last time I saw this play, which I had to when I was in high school, there was a lot of dueling. What is this, an adaptation where they cut out the dueling?

WALTER. Later. It comes later.

(Stage DARKENS.)

DONNA. Finally! I'm going to the bathroom.

MARGARET. I'll go see if they have a Danish.

WALTER. Will you both cool it? It's just the end of another scene. It's not an intermission. But if you really have to go the bathroom, you better go to the bathroom.

DONNA. I have to go to the bathroom. Where's the bathroom?

WALTER. May God forgive me. I forgot to notice where the ladies' toilet is.

MARGARET. You can ask an usher. You want me to go with you?

DONNA. You have to go to the bathroom, too?

MARGARET. I could use a bathroom. It's not an emergency, but I could use a bathroom. And I'll see if the refreshment counter has a Danish. Or a brownie would be all right.

(THEY stand up. Jewelry JANGLES.)

DONNA. Save our seats. We're going to the bathroom.

(THEY leave.)

WALTER. Peace and quiet.
STANLEY. What?
WALTER. I said peace and quiet.
STANLEY. What? Talk louder.
WALTER. I don't want to talk louder. I don't want to disturb people. Watch the play.
STANLEY. That's a good effect, that puff of smoke. How do they do that?
WALTER. They have what's called a smoke machine. They light it, and it makes smoke.
STANLEY. How do they get it to stop like that?
WALTER. They pour water on it.

(Pause.)

STANLEY. That's a long speech the ghost is making. He's just telling Hamlet how he died, right?
WALTER. Right. And he says Hamlet should kill his uncle but leave his mother alone.
STANLEY. Leave her to heaven! Did you hear that? Leave her to heaven! That was on TV the other night, on Film Classics. With what's her name and what's his name. They stole the title

from Shakespeare. That's very interesting. Probably his great-great-grandchildren, or whatever, get royalties on that.

WALTER. They're all dead.

STANLEY. Look, the swords! I told you there would be a duel.

WALTER. No, they're swearing. He's making them swear they won't say anything.

(LADIES return; jewelry JANGLES.)

MARGARET. What did we miss?

DONNA. Did we miss anything good?

STANLEY. There was this passionate love scene, and they all took off their clothes.

MARGARET. Don't you wish. What did we miss?

STANLEY. Nothing. The good part hasn't come yet.

MARGARET. What's the good part?

STANLEY. When they duel. Remember I told you about the duel?

MARGARET. How many acts does this thing have?

WALTER. Five. Every Shakespearean play has five acts.

STANLEY. Is that right? So we have five intermissions. That's clever. They can sell liquor during all five intermissions.

WALTER. Wrong. Think. Just think.

STANLEY. I'm not wrong. There's an intermission after each act, right? Five acts, five

intermissions. After Act I, there's an intermission. After Act II, there's an intermission. After Act III, there's an intermission. After Act IV, there's an intermission. And after Act V, —
WALTER. So, after Act V?
STANLEY. We go home. Okay, so there are four intermissions. So?
WALTER. You're still wrong, because there isn't an intermission after each act. That's not how it's done.
DONNA. What are they talking about?
MARGARET. Who? The people on stage?
DONNA. No. Who cares? What are the *boys* talking about?
MARGARET. About how many intermissions there are.
DONNA. Where's the program? We'll check in the program.

(RATTLING of paper.)

MARGARET. What does it say?
DONNA. I can't read a thing. It's dark in here.
STANLEY. At these prices, you'd think they would have enough light so people can read their programs.
WALTER. Everybody be quiet. This is one of my favorite parts.

(Pause.)

STANLEY. See how self-centered you are? *We* have to be quiet because it's one of *your* favorite parts. What about *my* favorite part?

MARGARET. I know what your favorite part is, Stanley, but you'll never see it on a stage, except in maybe a burlesque theater.

WALTER. Here it comes. Polonius's advice to Laertes.

STANLEY. Those are not Danish names.

WALTER. Listen. This is famous. You'll like this.

DONNA. I've heard this before. "Neither borrower nor lender be." I've heard that before.

(STANLEY noisily sneezes.)

MARGARET. Bless you.

DONNA. Gesundheit. Do you want a tissue? Here's a tissue.

(Loud RATTLING; STANLEY noisily blows his nose.)

WALTER. Stanley? Will you do me a favor? When we're in the theater, will you not sneeze so loudly? Will you please control your sneeze?

STANLEY. It's natural. Don't you ever sneeze? It's just a normal bodily function. Are you against normal bodily functions?

MARGARET. Isn't that beautiful? "To thine own self be true." That's the first thing I've liked.

But why are those two making fun of him? Are those his children?

WALTER. His two children.

STANLEY. They're making fun of him because he's pompous. He acts as if he knows it all. He really doesn't know anything. And he criticizes everyone. Nobody likes people like that.

DONNA. That's a pretty costume she has on.

MARGARET. It's nice, but it doesn't go with her hair. She should have something black. It would set off her hair better, don't you think?

DONNA. I think it's okay. What is that material? Is that taffeta? Her hair-do is pretty, but it's wrong. It doesn't frame her face.

STANLEY. She's got a nice build on her.

WALTER. How can you tell? That dress covers everything up.

STANLEY. I can tell. You have to know what to look for. She's got a nice build on her. What's her name? Is that Ophelia? Is that Hamlet's girlfriend?

WALTER. That's right.

STANLEY. Listen. What do you think of this? Ophelia, Ophelia, I want to feel ya.

WALTER. Brilliant.

STANLEY. Walter?

WALTER. What.

STANLEY. Is it true what you said before, about farmers putting cancer germs in their chickens?

WALTER. They don't anymore. The FAA has put a stop to it. I told you about that.

STANLEY. Why would farmers want to inject cancer germs in their chickens?

WALTER. Don't be so naive. It's greed. It's pure human greed. Isn't that obvious?

STANLEY. That's pretty obvious.

(Sound effect: ten seconds of loud beeping, tune of "Auld Lang Syne".)

WALTER. What in the world is that?

STANLEY. That's my new tech watch (shows it to Walter). Isn't it great? It can beep a lot of different tunes. Isn't that great? Besides "Auld Lang Syne," it can do "Jingle Bells," and it can do "Time on my Hands." You get it? "Time on My Hands." And it can do regular beeping. For example, it can beep five times at five o'clock, or six times at six o'clock, or seven times at seven o'clock. But I don't know how to program it yet. All I can get it to do is "Auld Lang Syne."

WALTER. It's too loud. Make it softer.

STANLEY. I can't. I told you. I don't know how to program it yet. The instructions are too hard. And it beeps at funny times. It's a good watch, but it doesn't tell time. *(Pause.)* Now what? Who are *they*?

WALTER. Rosencrantz and Guildenstern.

MARGARET. What did he say? Who are they?

STANLEY. He says they're Rosenkraut and Gildersleeve, or something.

WALTER. Rosencrantz and Guildenstern.

STANLEY. Which is which?

WALTER. It's not important.

STANLEY. You mean there's something about this play that the great expert can't figure out?

WALTER. You're not supposed to figure it out. It's not important. Shakespeare wants us to be confused about which is which.

STANLEY. Yeah, sure. Whenever you don't know something, you say it's not important. I don't know how Donna can put up with you.

WALTER. You know what? With all this talking and criticizing, I'm sorry we came. I should have come by myself. I should have gotten a single ticket.

STANLEY. Remember, it was your idea that the four of us should go someplace cultural together every week. Remember that?

WALTER. Of course I remember.

STANLEY. Remember who it was who started calling us the four musketeers? It was you. Remember you dragged us to the museum?

MARGARET. You know what this play is? Words, words, words.

WALTER. You just quoted something from the play.

MARGARET. What? What did you say?

WALTER. When you said "Words, words, words," that's from this play. In fact, it's coming soon.

MARGARET. I don't have any idea what you're talking about. Stanley, what's he talking about?

DONNA. I think we just missed something. People are laughing. What was so funny?

WALTER. Polonius is being made to appear ridiculous.

MARGARET. You know, we shouldn't have eaten Chinese before we came. It never agrees with me. It's all that MSG.

DONNA. You told them not to put any MSG in it, remember?

MARGARET. Sure, I remember. I think when you tell them not to put in any MSG, they put in twice as much. They don't like Americans. They take the MSG out of the food they give to their Chinese customers, and they give it to us. I'm feeling sweaty, and my right nostril feels paralyzed.

WALTER. What? Your nostrils are paralyzed?

MARGARET. Just my right nostril. I think it's from the MSG.

STANLEY. It's the Chinese waiters. They're trying to get rid of us. The whole Chinese government will take over the country. Have you seen all those Chinese tourists, with all those cameras? They're taking pictures of everything they own.

WALTER. That's Japanese tourists, not Chinese tourists.

STANLEY. Whatever. (*Pause.*) Did you hear that? Words, words, words.

MARGARET. That's right! Did you hear that? Words, words, words!

WALTER. That's right! That's right!

MARGARET. I was talking Shakespeare and I didn't know it.

DONNA. I think this would be a good thing to put on a record. It's all words. You don't have to go to a theater to hear words. You can just put on a record. And when you get tired of it, you can turn it off. Have they ever put this on a record?

WALTER. Yes. Many times.

DONNA. You see, I had a good idea.

WALTER. Brilliant.

MARGARET. Did I tell you Stanley and I got a new CD player?

DONNA. Stanley told me.

MARGARET. Stanley told you? When did Stanley tell you?

DONNA. Is that Hamlet? The one in the middle?

WALTER. Of course it's Hamlet. I told you a long time ago that was Hamlet. Who else would it be? If you paid attention, you would know that's Hamlet.

DONNA. I think he's Jewish.

MARGARET. Hamlet is Jewish?

DONNA. No, the actor. The actor who's playing him, I think he's Jewish.

MARGARET. Why?

DONNA. He looks Jewish to me. Stanley, what's his name? That actor?

STANLEY. I don't remember. Ask Walter.

DONNA. I don't want to disturb him. You know how he gets.

STANLEY. You're afraid of him? You're afraid of Walter?

DONNA. No. I'm not afraid of him. I'm just afraid of his anger.

STANLEY. That's the same thing.

DONNA. No, it isn't. Look how sweet he looks when he's concentrating. I don't want to disturb him. (*Pause.*) Walter, what's the name of that actor? Is it a Jewish name?

WALTER. Can't you wait?

DONNA. No. It's important.

WALTER. I'll check.

(*RUSTLING of program.*)

DONNA. What's his name? Can you read it?

WALTER. If I twist a little, I can read it. (*He twists.*) Now I can read it. His name is —

(*Note: If the first staging alternative has been selected, the actor who is miming Hamlet's part will be identified in the program. There are three possible scenarios at this point, depending on the actor's name. Here are examples of each. If the second or third staging alternative is selected, the third scenario [below] should be used.*)

(1)

WALTER. Goldman. Steven Goldman.

DONNA. See? I told you he was Jewish.

STANLEY. Goldman doesn't have to be Jewish. It could be German.

DONNA. No, he's definitely Jewish.
(2)
WALTER. Kelly. His name is Kelly.
DONNA. That's probably just his stage name. They all do that. He changed it from a Jewish name so he could get more parts. He's definitely Jewish.
(3)
WALTER. Burke.
STANLEY. That's not a Jewish name.
DONNA. It could be from Berkowitz. They do that a lot. They Americanize their names. You know Barbara and Joe? Their real name isn't Green. It's Greenblatt. Did you know that?

DONNA. Who has the binoculars? I want to look at him with the binoculars.
WALTER. I gave them to Margaret to use.
MARGARET. I have them. Here.

(MARGARET hands them to DONNA.)

DONNA. They're broken. I can't see anything. Everything is out of focus.
STANLEY. You have to adjust them.
DONNA. What do I turn? What do I have to turn?
STANLEY. Walter, how do you adjust your binoculars?
WALTER. That little knob. See the little knob? Turn the little knob.

DONNA. Where's the little knob? *(Loud crash.)* Oh, no! I dropped them!

WALTER. You dropped my binoculars? My three-hundred-dollar binoculars?

DONNA. They didn't fall very far. I can get them. *(Gets on floor.)*

STANLEY. What are you doing? What is she doing?

WALTER. She's looking for my three-hundred-dollar binoculars, which she dropped on the floor.

DONNA. Here they are. No. This is something else. Oh, my goodness. It's somebody's purse. I picked up somebody's purse! What should I do?

WALTER. Just put it back on the floor. You can get the binoculars during intermission.

DONNA. Okay. That's a good idea. There ought to be an intermission soon.

(Pause.
DONNA squirms. Jewelry JANGLES.)

STANLEY. What are you doing?

DONNA. I think I can feel the strap with my feet. Yes, I can feel it. I can pick them up with my feet. *(Squirming.)* Here, Walter. They seem bent. I think they were broken because you gave them to me.

WALTER. Sure. Thanks a lot.

(Pause.)

MARGARET. Those are cute outfits. Who are they?

WALTER. Those are the actors.

MARGARET. Of course they're the actors. All of them are the actors. Don't be funny.

WALTER. No, these are actors playing the role of actors. See that guy dressed in women's clothes? In those days, women's parts were played by men.

MARGARET. Is he gay? He must be gay. That's disgusting.

(Pause.)

STANLEY. What was that all about? That was the longest speech in the whole damned play, and I didn't understand a word.

WALTER. Later. I'll explain it later. Maybe we'll go someplace and I'll explain the whole play.

STANLEY. I don't want you to explain the whole play. I understand the whole play. I just want to know what they were just talking about.

WALTER. Later.

(Applause.)

STANLEY. Is that it? Is it over?

WALTER. You're joking. You're just kidding, aren't you? It's intermission.

STANLEY. Of course I was kidding. Everybody knows it's intermission.

DONNA. Did you hear that, Margaret? It's intermission.

MARGARET. Thank God.

(For first staging alternative, mimes bow.)

WALTER. Donna, are you applauding? Why are you applauding? You paid very little attention, when you did pay attention you didn't understand most of it, and when you did understand it you didn't like it. So why are you clapping?

DONNA. Out of courtesy. To make the performers feel good. To make them think they did a good job. That's just common courtesy. And you know? I'm actually glad I came. I think it's good to go to a Shakespeare play once in a while. Walter, if this is still playing next week, let's suggest to Jennifer that she should go.

WALTER. Suggest? What suggest? We'll *tell* her. We'll tell her she has to come see this. It'll be good for her. It'll broaden her mind.

DONNA. Well, I don't think we should order her —

WALTER. That's the whole trouble. You're too soft on her. You handle her with kid gloves. She needs discipline.

DONNA. She doesn't need discipline. She has too much discipline. She's a sensitive child.

WALTER. Too much discipline? Nineteen years old and she's already flunked out of three colleges. That's discipline? Don't make me laugh.

(Sound effect: again ten seconds of "Auld Lang Syne".)

WALTER. Not again!

STANLEY. It's supposed to beep every hour on the hour.

WALTER. It beeped just ten minutes ago. Why is it beeping now? It's *(looks at his watch)* not on the hour. It's *(says correct time)*. Why is it beeping now?

STANLEY. I told you. I don't know how to program it.

WALTER. How much did you pay for that watch?

STANLEY. A hundred dollars. The guy who sold it to me, he said it was made in Switzerland. It's a Swiss watch.

WALTER. If you give it to me right now, I'll write you a check for a hundred twenty.

STANLEY. You mean it?

WALTER. *(Takes out his checkbook.)* I mean it.

STANLEY. Okay. You must really like it.

(STANLEY hands watch to WALTER, who writes a check and hands it to STANLEY. WALTER puts watch on floor, stands up, jumps on watch.)

WALTER. The time is out of joint!

STANLEY. What are you doing? Are you crazy? Is he crazy?

MARGARET. What's he doing? Why is he jumping up and down like that?

STANLEY. He's nuts. He just ruined the watch I paid a hundred bucks for.

MARGARET. A hundred dollars? You just paid twenty dollars for it when you bought it from that man who was selling watches on the corner. Remember?

STANLEY. Be quiet. Can't you just be quiet?

DONNA. On one of my shows, they said Swiss watches aren't made in Switzerland. They're made by prisoners in Cuba or someplace.

STANLEY. Who cares? Let's go out to the lobby. I want to stretch my legs.

DONNA. Do they have refreshments out there? I'm starving. Are you starving? I'm starving.

WALTER. You ate two hours ago. You're not hungry.

DONNA. Don't tell me I'm not hungry. You think you know what goes on in my body? You don't know anything what goes on in my body. *Anything.* It seems like two weeks since we ate. This is a long play. I suppose we all want to come back and see how it ends?

WALTER. I *know* how it ends. Everybody knows how it ends. You don't watch it to see how it ends. Football games you watch to see how they end.

MARGARET. So why do you watch it if you know how it ends?

WALTER. To see how they do it. To see how the actors act and how the director directs.

DONNA. I like to see how the audience reacts. That person over there, on the right? With the ugly brown suit?

MARGARET. Where? With the glasses?

DONNA. No, in front of him. One, two, three rows in front of him. Do you see him?

MARGARET. Yes. What about him?

DONNA. He was sleeping. You think *Stanley* sleeps? That guy slept through the whole thing. Can you imagine spending good money to come see *Macbeth* and sleeping through it? I was watching him the whole time, and all he did was sleep.

WALTER. *Hamlet.* This is *Hamlet.*

DONNA. *Hamlet, Macbeth,* what's the difference? Don't get so excited. Stanley, what do you think of this so far? Do you like it?

STANLEY. The sets aren't very fancy. They're a little chintzy, you know what I mean? I like them fancy. Remember when we saw "Les Miz"? (*HE pronounces it "Less Miz.")*

WALTER. It's not "Less Miz." Don't you know any French? The s's are always silent. It's "Lay Miz."

STANLEY. If the s's are always silent, it should be "Lay *Me.*"

MARGARET. What are you saying, Stanley?

STANLEY. Lay *me.* Lay *me.*

MARGARET. Stop that! You're embarrassing me!

DONNA. (*Stands up, JANGLING.*) Let's go for a stretch.

MARGARET. (*Stands up.*) I want to ask you something. You said Stanley told you about our new CD player? How could he tell you when we just got it yesterday? When did he talk to you?

DONNA. I made a mistake. He didn't tell me.

MARGARET. Then how did you —

STANLEY. Are you girls just going to stand here? Do you want to walk around or do you want to sit down? You can't just stand there like that.

DONNA. Let's go walk around. I want to walk around.

STANLEY. Let's all walk around. Walter, you want to walk around?

WALTER. I'll stay here. I want to read the notes in the program. They tell about the background of the play.

STANLEY. Nobody reads that stuff. Come on and stretch your legs. You can read that stuff later.

WALTER. Okay. I could use a stretch.

STANLEY. You want to take a leak, Walter? Let's go take a leak.

(For Staging Alternatives 2 and 3, ALL exit.)

ACT II

(ALL FOUR return but do not sit down.)

DONNA. So what do you think? You want to keep these seats or do you want to move up? We can move up if we want to. I saw some empty seats. Can you see okay from here, or do you want to move up?

MARGARET. You know what I think? I think the people who were sitting in front of us have left, or they've changed their seats. Can you imagine that?

DONNA. Maybe they just haven't come back from intermission.

MARGARET. I don't think they're coming back. You see they didn't leave their coats or programs or anything. Can you imagine spending so much money for tickets and then leaving in the middle? I didn't like those people, anyway. Did you notice how they kept turning around and looking at us, and glaring? Did you see how rude they were?

WALTER. You were talking too loud. You were talking too loud, so they glared.

MARGARET. That's real nerve. I paid my money, I can talk as loud as I want to.

DONNA. You know, I think the people behind us aren't coming back either. There's nobody in front of us and nobody behind us. I think we should stay here. So there won't be anybody to disturb us.

(LIGHTS dim.)

WALTER. The lights are going out. Let's sit down.

MARGARET. Let's sit down.

(THEY sit.)

STANLEY. What happens in this act? Doesn't Ophelia go nuts? I seem to remember Ophelia goes nuts. Or is it the mother who goes nuts? Somebody goes nuts.

DONNA. I think Hamlet is the nutty one. Talking to himself like that.

WALTER. Quiet. It's beginning soon.

MARGARET. I feel a draft. Do you feel a draft?

WALTER. Quiet. You can feel a draft later.

(Stage LIGHTS brighten.)

DONNA. It's those two stupid guys again. I don't like them. They have such drab outfits.

MARGARET. They're talking about Hamlet. They're telling the King something about Hamlet.

DONNA. What about Hamlet?

MARGARET. I don't know. But it's something about Hamlet, I know that.

DONNA. There's Ophelia. Look, she changed clothes. That's cut a little low, don't you think?

MARGARET. Don't ask Stanley. He probably likes it. It's probably the highlight of the play for Stanley. If it was cut all the way to her crotch, then he would *really* like it. Then this would be his favorite play.

STANLEY. I know this part. To be or not to be, that is the question.

WALTER. Let the actor do it. He gets paid to do it. Are you trying to show off, or what?

STANLEY. Me? No, I'm not trying to show off. I think you're a little out of line when you say that. You're the showoff.

(Pause.)

DONNA. That's famous isn't it? Does it mean he wants to kill himself? I don't understand Shakespeare at all. They're all so long-winded.

(Pause.)

STANLEY. What did he say?

WALTER. The proud man's contumely.

STANLEY. What?

WALTER. The proud man's contumely.

STANLEY. The proud man's what?

WALTER. Contumely.

STANLEY. Contumely? What's that?

WALTER. You should know that. Every educated person knows what contumely means.

STANLEY. So educate me. What does it mean?

WALTER. I'll tell you later. Let's not talk during the play.

(Pause.)

MARGARET. Here comes that Ophelia again. Isn't she cute? I like her. She's giving him something. Is that a present?
DONNA. I don't know. Stanley, what is she giving him?
STANLEY. Don't ask me — ask the expert. Walter's the expert.
MARGARET. I figured it out. She's giving him back some gifts he gave her. She's breaking up with him.
DONNA. It's about time. She can do better. I don't like how he treats her. He shows contempt for her. He doesn't respect her. If she respects herself, she shouldn't put up with that. Women never show contempt for women. It's only men who show contempt for women.
MARGARET. Listen! Did you hear what he said? He wants her to go to a nunnery. Did you hear that? I guess he's saying that if he can't have her, he doesn't want anyone else to. He's very possessive. That's love. It shows he still loves her. When you love somebody, you want him all to yourself. I wouldn't share my Stanley with anybody. If he had a little girlfriend on the side, I think I'd kill them both. I'd kill her, and I'd kill him. Then I'd kill myself.

(Pause.)

DONNA. See how he waves his arms? That's cute.

MARGARET. What did you say? Those people on the stage are talking so loud I can't hear you.

DONNA. I said it's cute, the way he waves his arms like that.

(Pause.
STANLEY yawns loudly.)

WALTER. Stanley? May I tell you something?

STANLEY. Sure. What?

WALTER. I'm not enjoying this play because you're ruining it.

STANLEY. Ruin it? How I am ruining it?

WALTER. You talk loud. You make stupid comments. You sneeze so loudly that everybody in the theater is disturbed. You yawn like a jerk. You're behaving like a jerk. You're not considerate. Look at me — I'm starting to talk loud, too. Your jerkiness is contagious.

STANLEY. I've paid my money, and —

WALTER. I made a mistake. You're not just *behaving* like a jerk. You actually *are* a jerk. I've suspected it for years. I wouldn't let myself realize it, because you're my best friend. But now I realize it. You are a jerk. You are a real jerk. Now I know why Margaret ...

STANLEY. Why Margaret what?

WALTER. Nothing.

STANLEY. Why Margaret what?

WALTER. Why Margaret looks embarrassed. You embarrass her, because you're such a jerk, that's all.

STANLEY. You're in a cruddy mood, aren't you? Something's bugging you, and you're taking it out on me. What's the matter? Did you and Donna have another fight?

WALTER. Another fight? What do you mean "another"?

STANLEY. Don't bother me. I want to see the play. This is Shakespeare.

MARGARET. What did he say?

WALTER. He said we should pay attention to the play. He's right, for a change. All of you have been yackity-yacking since we got here. You're supposed to come to the theater for intellectual stimulation.

DONNA. Intellectual stimulation? Oh, *please*. I don't go to the theater for intellectual stimulation. I go to relax and to chat with my friends. If I want intellectual stimulation, I watch my shows. Yesterday, for instance, there was this psychologist guy who said that marriage is a bad thing and should be abolished.

MARGARET. He must be gay.

DONNA. Who? The psychologist guy?

MARGARET. Anybody who is against marriage must be gay.

DONNA. Oh, *please*. You think everybody is gay. On one of my other shows, they said that people who think everybody is gay is actually gay.

STANLEY. Who said that?

DONNA. I don't remember. It was either a celebrity or an authority. I can't tell the difference.

MARGARET. Are you saying I'm a lesbian, Donna?

DONNA. No, I'm not saying that, because I'm not a lesbian.

(Pause.)

MARGARET. Did you hear that? He fluffed his line, didn't he? Did you hear that, Walter?

WALTER. I heard it. I heard it.

STANLEY. With all the money we pay for the tickets, we have a right to have actors who don't mess up their lines.

MARGARET. You look very angry, Stanley. What's the matter?

WALTER. I think he's insulted.

MARGARET. Why is he insulted?

WALTER. I told him he's a jerk.

MARGARET. He's not insulted. He never cares what you say. (*Pause.*) I'm freezing. Stanley, let me have your jacket.

STANLEY. You want my jacket? (*Stands up, removes jacket, gives to Margaret.*)

MARGARET. Thank you. (*Stands up, puts on jacket.*)

WALTER. This is an important part. It's the play within the play.

DONNA. The play within the play? Who ever heard of a play inside another play? That's stupid.

Is this one of those experimental plays? I don't like experimental plays.
    WALTER. No, it's not an experimental play.

(Pause.
LIGHTS dim.)

    MARGARET. Why did they play that music? Why are all those people there?
    DONNA. Walter says it's a play within a play, or something.
    MARGARET. Oh.

(Stage LIGHTS brighten. STANLEY stands up.)

    WALTER. Sit down, Stanley.
    STANLEY. They just turned on the lights.
    WALTER. The king said to turn on the lights. That's all. Sit down.

(STANLEY sits.)

    DONNA. Why is Hamlet acting like that?
    MARGARET. I think it means he really liked that little play they put on.
    DONNA. It was short. That's why he liked it.
    MARGARET. Oh, look. Here comes that funny guy again. I like him. (*Long pause.)* Do you like this play?
    DONNA. What?
    MARGARET. Do you like this, what we're watching?

DONNA. It's okay. Did you mean it, what you said before, about killing Stanley if he was unfaithful?

MARGARET. I don't have to worry about that. I give him everything he wants.

DONNA. Even if you do, maybe he just wants a change once in a while. Stanley, is that right? Margaret says she gives you everything you want. She says she has nothing to worry about. Is that right?

WALTER. What are you doing? Are you propositioning Stanley? She's propositioning you, Stan. You better be careful. If you have an affair with her, I might have an affair with Margaret.

MARGARET. What did he say?

DONNA. Something about having an affair with you.

MARGARET. He said that? He said that? He told — He said that?

DONNA. He was joking. That's his idea of a joke.

MARGARET. Of course he was joking. Who said he wasn't joking? Let's watch the play.

(Pause.)

DONNA. Margaret?

MARGARET. What.

DONNA. He *was* joking, wasn't he?

MARGARET. Who? Walter? What's the matter? You don't trust your own husband? You think he'd cheat on you? You don't trust me? You think I

would do something like that? We're best friends.
Would I do that to you?

WALTER. What are they yacking about now?

STANLEY. Don't ask me. Ask them. You think
I know everything? I don't know everything.

(Pause.)

WALTER. Listen. Hamlet is telling Horatio
about the play-within-the-play.

MARGARET. *(to Donna.)* They're talking too
loud again. I can't hear what Walter said. Will you
ask Stanley what Walter said?

DONNA. *(to Stanley.)* What did Walter say?

STANLEY. *(to Walter.)* What did you say? They
want to know what you said.

WALTER. *(to Stanley.)* I said he's telling
Horatio about the play.

STANLEY. *(looks at Walter. uncomprehendingly. shrugs, turns to Donna.)* Something about he
tells him to pay.

DONNA. *(looks at Stanley. uncomprehendingly.
shrugs, turns to Margaret.)* He sells a toupée.
Something like that.

(DONNA shrugs.)

MARGARET. *(to the other three.)* It's not a swell
toupée. It's very scraggly.

*(WALTER, STANLEY and DONNA stare at
    MARGARET.
Pause.)*

WALTER. Here comes the closet scene.

STANLEY. The closet scene?

WALTER. That's just what they call it. It's not really a closet. It's Gertrude's bedroom. The queen's bedroom. It's a very dramatic scene.

(Pause.)

MARGARET. *(Gasping.)* Did you see that? The crazy nut stabbed that other guy.

STANLEY. It's his own fault for snooping. He shouldn't have been hiding behind the curtain. Sometimes when you're too curious, bad things can happen.

MARGARET. What's *that* supposed to mean?

STANLEY. Nothing.

MARGARET. Stanley? *(No response.)* Stanley?

STANLEY. Now what? You want to go to the toilet again?

MARGARET. Stanley, I know this isn't a good time to ask, but I have to ask.

STANLEY. Ask what?

MARGARET. Donna said some interesting things. Stanley, are you having an affair?

STANLEY. *(After a pause.)* You're asking me now, in the middle of *Hamlet,* if I'm having an affair? What's the matter with you?

MARGARET. Yes, I'm asking you now.

STANLEY. You're asking me in front of Donna and Walter?

MARGARET. Well, *are* you?

STANLEY. I think you're cracking up. You're insecure. Only an insecure person would ask her husband a question like that. Especially in the middle of *Hamlet*. What's the matter with you?

MARGARET. You're not answering me. Why aren't you answering me?

STANLEY. I *did* answer you. Pay attention. I said it was a ridiculous question. What else do you want me to say?

MARGARET. Are you having an affair with Donna?

STANLEY. With Donna? Who told you with Donna? One of your stupid little friends? What's gotten into you? I'll tell you something. You start planting ideas in my head like that, I might just go ahead and *have* an affair with Donna. And don't blame me if it happens. You understand? Now watch the play. I'm beginning to be sorry we came. This is a great play and look what you're doing. You're ruining the whole play. Look how he's grabbing his mother's wrist. That's good. Walter, is he going to kill her?

WALTER. No, the ghost will come and stop him. See? There's the ghost.

DONNA. Did you hear what she said, what the queen said? She says she can't see the ghost. How can she not see the ghost when *we* can see him? He's right there.

STANLEY. Maybe it's a hallucination.

WALTER. If it's a hallucination, how come *we* can see it? You're not thinking.

STANLEY. Mr. Know-it-all. You don't know everything. There are some things you don't know.

WALTER. What do you mean?

STANLEY. Just what I said. There are some things you don't know.

WALTER. I know that. I never said I know everything.

STANLEY. Then why do you act as if you do?

WALTER. I don't.

STANLEY. Remember the concert last week? Remember how you showed off? You call me a showoff, and you're the real showoff.

WALTER. Showed off? I didn't show off. How did I show off?

STANLEY. You showed off. Remember how you closed your eyes like that, pretending you were conducting? That really got to me.

WALTER. That wasn't showing off. I never show off. I was just involved in the music. I was expressing myself.

STANLEY. Sure.

WALTER. If it bothers you so much, go to your next concert without me.

STANLEY. I never go to concerts without you. You're the only one who drags us to these places. I wouldn't be surprised if one of these times you'll drag us to a ballet.

WALTER. You never complained about this to me before.

STANLEY. Whenever anybody tells you how egotistical you are, you blow up. Donna agrees with me.

WALTER. Donna? *My* Donna? You talk about me to Donna? When do you talk to her about me?

STANLEY. When? When? How do I remember when? Different times. On the telephone. It must have been on the telephone. I don't remember. It's not important.

WALTER. You talk to Donna on the telephone?

STANLEY. What's happening now? What are they doing?

WALTER. He's pulling out Polonius's body. We have to talk later.

DONNA. I don't understand what's so great about Shakespeare. Is this supposed to be a great play? This isn't holding my interest. Neil Simon holds my interest. Margaret, is this holding your interest?

MARGARET. This is a classic. Of course it's holding my interest. If you're intelligent, it holds your interest. That's how you know you're intelligent: if a classic holds your interest. You're comparing Shakespeare to Neil Simon?

DONNA. Are you saying something about my intelligence? Is that what you're doing? Smarty, there's a Broadway theater named after Neil Simon. Is there a theater named after Shakespeare?

MARGARET. Listen. Did you hear what he said? He said he's going to England. Did I tell you that Stanley and I are going to England?

DONNA. That should be a wonderful trip. London, and then on to Scotland ...

MARGARET. Scotland? How did you know about Scotland? We just decided about Scotland a few days ago.

DONNA. You must have told me.

MARGARET. I haven't spoken to you since we decided. The last I spoke to you was before we decided.

DONNA. I must have just guessed. It's a natural thing to guess. Everybody who goes to London goes to Scotland.

(Pause.
DONNA jangles.)

WALTER. Donna, please. It sounds like a cowbell.

DONNA. I can't help it. I'm restless.

STANLEY. What's happening now? I'm lost.

WALTER. You see the position you put me in? This is an impossible position. If I tell you what's happening, then I'm showing off. So don't ask me.

STANLEY. Just tell me what's happening. Don't make a federal case out of it.

WALTER. That other character's name is Fortinbras. He's leading his troops into battle for a stupid reason, just to get some land. And Hamlet says that these soldiers are willing to die for no good reason, while he doesn't have the courage to kill his father. This is an anti-war play.

STANLEY. This could be a good play if it were a little shorter.

WALTER. It *is* a little shorter.

STANLEY. What?

WALTER. They've made some cuts.

STANLEY. They made cuts? We pay full price and they made cuts? They're a bunch of shysters. Everybody in the theater business is a shyster. I think we can get everybody here to file a class-action suit. This is gross misrepresentation. First we'll set up a petition —

WALTER. You just said you thought it was too long, and now you're complaining —

STANLEY. I think next time I go to a play, I won't go with you.

WALTER. Fine. That's fine.

STANLEY. You always put me down. I'll go with somebody else.

WALTER. Fine.

MARGARET. Stanley, your jacket keeps me warm, pretty much, but it irritates my skin. You know I have hypersensitive skin. It's very hyper-sensitive. But if I take off your jacket, I'll get a chill. Will you tell them to turn the heat up?

STANLEY. No.

MARGARET. You never do anything I ask you to.

STANLEY. Watch the play. Why is she singing like that? She's singing like a madwoman.

MARGARET. That's a cute song.

DONNA. I think when the play's over, we have to talk.

STANLEY. Did you hear that? When the play's over, Margaret and Donna want to talk.

WALTER. That's all they've been doing since we got here.

STANLEY. I think it's something important.

WALTER. What could be so important? Look. Here comes Laertes. He's furious because his father has been killed. He behaves the way Hamlet would like to behave but can't.

STANLEY. His father has been killed? Who's his father?

WALTER. I don't believe this. Polonius was his father. The guy who was killed behind the curtain. Where have you been?

STANLEY. I knew that.

WALTER. Sure you did.

DONNA. This is getting dramatic. It's more interesting now.

MARGARET. What do you want to talk about?

DONNA. Different things. Not now. Later.

(Pause.)

MARGARET. Did you hear that? Ophelia drowned.

DONNA. Is *that* what they're talking about? I wondered what that was all about. They should have shown her drowning. That would have been more dramatic. After all, this is a theater. If all they do is talk, we can listen on the radio or on a record.

WALTER. You said that before.

DONNA. So I'm saying it again. Okay?

STANLEY. Go easy on her, Walter.

WALTER. Don't tell me how to handle my wife. I know how to handle my wife.
STANLEY. Sure you do.

(Pause.)

DONNA. What's that? Is that a grave? Those are grave diggers. I think those are grave diggers. Look. They're digging a grave.
MARGARET. That must be for Hamlet. Did he die already? I missed that part. We must be near the end.
STANLEY. Don't be stupid. That's not for Hamlet. I think that's for Polonius.
MARGARET. Which one was he?
STANLEY. Don't you remember? He got stabbed. Do I have to explain everything?
MARGARET. They seem to be telling jokes. People are laughing. Look. Hamlet is there. You were right. He didn't die yet. Is that Hamlet?

(Pause.)

DONNA. Look at that. You know what Jennifer would say? She would say that's gross. She thinks skeletons and things like that are gross. Whose skull is that? Did you say it belonged to Polonius?
STANLEY. I think so. I think that's his grave. But he lost his skin very quickly. I don't know how long it takes a body to rot. I'll bet Walter knows.
DONNA. There are a lot of things Walter doesn't know.

MARGARET. Like what?

(Pause.)

DONNA. Look at that. It's like a funeral procession. See? There's the priest. See the priest? He looks familiar. Wasn't he somebody else before?
WALTER. Sometimes one actor has two roles. That's called dovetailing.
DONNA. Look. The Queen is crying. She's a good actress. Those look like real tears.
STANLEY. They do that with onions.
DONNA. Who's that?
WALTER. That's Laertes. You probably don't know who Laertes is.
DONNA. Of course I do. I'm not stupid. Did you hear that, Margaret? That's Laertes or something. Do you remember who he is?
MARGARET. It sounds familiar. It sounds very familiar. Does it sound familiar to you?
DONNA. Sort of. Look! Look! He jumped in! That's dramatic. Why didn't they do something like that a long time ago?
STANLEY. This is a good scene. It has comedy, and it has jumping.
WALTER. Comedy and jumping. If it has comedy and jumping, it's a good scene.
STANLEY. Well, it is.

*(Pause.
LIGHTS dim.)*

MARGARET. It's dark again. So that means a new act is beginning, or what? This must be near the end. Where do you want to go after this?

DONNA. Where we can talk. Somewhere where we can talk.

MARGARET. Look at that guy. Look how he simpers there, with his hat. Do you see that, Stanley? See how he simpers? I hate that.

STANLEY. He's funny. I think he's supposed to be funny. I'll ask Walter if he's supposed to be—

MARGARET. I think he's gay. He looks gay to me. That's disgusting. People can do whatever they want, but gay, that's disgusting. That's going too far. God punished them by giving them AIDS.

DONNA. Oh, please. Don't be ridiculous, Margaret. There are a lot of people who have AIDS without being gay.

MARGARET. God's punishing *them,* too. They must have sinned somehow.

DONNA. Oh, please. You mean an innocent child who gets it from a blood transfusion? You mean God knows that child did something wrong and should die of AIDS? Are you serious?

MARGARET. God knows everything. Otherwise they wouldn't call him "God." He would just be an angel or a saint.

(Pause.)

WALTER. Shhh. Look what's happening.

STANLEY. At last. The duel. Be quiet, everybody. I want to see this.

MARGARET. That looks very realistic.

DONNA. Did you read where there was an actor who actually stabbed another actor on stage? I think it was in *Hamlet*. I heard he did it on purpose.

MARGARET. Yes, I read that. That was interesting. It was in a magazine. His name was — What was his name? Nichols. William Nichols.

DONNA. Wasn't he in *Lawrence of Arabia*? With the blue eyes?

STANLEY. No, that was somebody else. Peter something. It wasn't William Nichols.

WALTER. Nicol Williamson! Nicol Williamson!

STANLEY. You did it again. Why do you have to show off? Why do you have to say it so loud that everybody in the theater hears you? Is it really so important that everybody knows how smart you are?

DONNA. Really, Walter, you're embarrassing me. One of my shows explained that when a man shows off like that, it means he's insecure. They have doubts about their manhood. You're like a little boy showing off how much you know. There's a lot you don't know.

WALTER. You said that before.

DONNA. There's a lot you don't know.

STANLEY. Will the two of you stop talking already? This is the duel. I'm watching the duel. Watch the duel.

DONNA. Look! He just got killed. It must be almost over. When the main character dies, the

play is almost over. Was that Hamlet who died?
Let's leave so we can avoid the crowd.

WALTER. That's very discourteous. It's
discourteous to the performers, and it's
discourteous to the audience. Sit down till it's over.

MARGARET. He isn't dead. Look what he's
doing. He's talking. Remember that opera, when
the woman took a half hour to die? Look. He's
talking to his mother. Look how she keeled over.
She must be sad because her son is dying. That *is*
her son, isn't it? It's like Mary and Jesus. This
play is like Mary and Jesus. I just thought of that.

STANLEY. Jeez, look at all the corpses. There
must be ten dead people out there. This is a real
tragedy.

WALTER. Yes. Yes, Stanley. This is a real
tragedy.

(Pause.)

STANLEY. Who's that?

WALTER. Are you asking me?

STANLEY. Sure I'm asking you. I just asked
you.

WALTER. Are you really asking me?

STANLEY. Forget it. Just forget it.

WALTER. Fortinbras. You have probably never
heard of him.

(LIGHTS dim.)

DONNA. It's dark again. Don't tell me there's another act. I don't think I can handle another act.

(APPLAUSE.)

MARGARET. People are clapping. It's over. We did it. We sat through the whole thing.

(For the first alternative of staging, the mimes bow and exit.)

STANLEY. (*Yells.*) Bravo!
WALTER. Bravo? You're yelling bravo?
STANLEY. That was a good duel. That was a realistic duel.
WALTER. Let's get out of here.
DONNA. So are we going to go someplace to talk? I think we have a lot to talk about.
MARGARET. Not now. It's late. I'm tired.
DONNA. I'm tired, too. We don't have to talk right now. Where are we going next week? Wherever we're going, we can eat first, and we can get together and talk. Where do we have to go next week?
MARGARET. An opera, I think. Isn't it next week that we have to go to the opera again? I don't remember what opera we're going to. We could go to that Italian place where they dropped the plates. The food isn't too bad. But it's too noisy. I have hypersensitive hearing. We want to go someplace quiet where we can talk. I suppose we could talk at the opera, but sometimes those

singers scream their heads off. Where do *you* want to go to eat next week, Stanley?

STANLEY. I don't know and I don't care. What do we have to see next week?

WALTER. *Fidelio*. We're going to see *Fidelio* next week.

STANLEY. Since it's Italian, we might as well eat Italian.

WALTER. It isn't Italian. It's German.

STANLEY. "Fidelio" doesn't sound German. It's either Italian or Puerto Rican. What is it? An opera, or a play?

WALTER. It's an opera. You never heard of *Fidelio*?

STANLEY. Of course I have. I was joking.

WALTER. Sure you were. Besides, you said before you didn't want to go anyplace with us again.

STANLEY. With *you*. I don't want to go anyplace with *you* again.

WALTER. That's what I said.

STANLEY. You said us. You and Donna haven't been an us for years.

WALTER. What do you know about Donna and me?

DONNA. Come on, you two. You're both getting excited. We're out to have a good time. Let's go have a quick cup of coffee.

WALTER. Okay. We can talk about the play.

STANLEY. What's to talk about? It's a simple play. I had to read it in high school. If it was so complicated, they wouldn't make you read it in high school.

MARGARET. Well, are we going or not? Don't you want to beat the rush?

WALTER. The rush has already begun. Let's sit here until all the other people have left.

DONNA. He always does that. On airplanes, when everybody else is in the aisle waiting to get out, he's still sitting there, reading.

WALTER. It makes sense, doesn't it? Let's talk about the play here, while it's still fresh in our minds. Stanley, what do you think the play's about?

STANLEY. What? You mean *Hamlet*?

WALTER. No. *Cyrano de Bergerac*. Of course I mean *Hamlet*.

STANLEY. What's it about? It's about Hamlet.

MARGARET. Don't be so superficial. He means what's the theme. What's the moral.

STANLEY. Smarty, you tell me. What's it about?

MARGARET. I missed too many lines. They didn't speak clearly enough. Maybe we should have sat closer. We should have bought more expensive tickets. But if we sat closer, we would see them spit. If something is expensive, it isn't worth it, and if something is cheap, it isn't any good.

STANLEY. You have very superficial values.

MARGARET. What do you mean, superficial values?

DONNA. Walter, while they're talking, I have to ask you something. It's important.

WALTER. What's so important?

DONNA. Margaret has been saying things that make me curious. They make me suspicious. Walter, tell me the truth. Are you having an affair with Margaret?

WALTER. That's a ridiculous question. That's the most stupid question you've ever asked me.

DONNA. It's not so ridiculous, because Margaret said —

WALTER. Listen. If I've been having an affair with Margaret, that would make me a deceitful and dishonest person, wouldn't it?

DONNA. That's right.

WALTER. If I'm a deceitful and dishonest person, if you asked me if I had an affair, would I tell you the truth? Of course not. I would lie. You see what a stupid question you asked?

DONNA. You're right. That was a stupid question. I don't know why I always say such stupid things. I'm sorry.

WALTER. I'll overlook it this time. Next time, use your head. Quiet. They're finished talking.

STANLEY. Walter, did you hear what Margaret said? She's sorry she came because she didn't get much out of it.

WALTER. What? You mean you didn't get anything out of the play at all? You sat here all this time and didn't get anything out of it? I don't believe it. You're hopeless. You're as hopeless as Donna.

MARGARET. Wait a minute.

WALTER. What's the matter?

MARGARET. Don't talk to me like that. You can talk to Donna like that because she's your wife. Stanley can talk to *me* like that because I'm *his* wife. But you must not talk to me like that. Stop putting me down like that, or ...

WALTER. Or what?

MARGARET. Or else.

WALTER. Everybody's out to get me tonight. Hamlet has done something to all of you. I don't know why. It's this play. I made a mistake about our coming to see it. Maybe a tragedy makes people see the bad things in the world. All of us. Comedies make us forget about all the rotten things in the world and in ourselves, and tragedies make us remember. Okay, I'm sorry. I shouldn't have put you down. I apologize. So let's have an ordinary conversation. So what did you think of the play?

MARGARET. I understood part of it. You want me to tell you what I think it was about? It was about love. Remember how he treated Ophelia? He treated her badly like that because he loved her. Remember when he jumped into the grave? That's how much he loved her. It's a tragedy about love. Remember when we saw *Romeo and Juliet* that time? After that Italian restaurant where the waitress dropped all those plates? *Romeo and Juliet* was another tragedy about love. Shakespeare writes tragedies about love.

DONNA. That's the trouble with you, Margaret. You're sentimental. *Romeo and Juliet* was about love, but *Hamlet* is different. *Hamlet* is deeper than that. *Hamlet* is about hate. Everybody hates everybody. Didn't you notice that? Hamlet was so sarcastic! And then he killed that old man, and at the end he killed that other old man? It's about the younger generation hating the older generation. It's like with Jennifer. Yesterday, or two days ago it was, when I told her she had to clean up her room before she could use the car, she said she hated me. Remember, Walter?

WALTER. Of course I remember.

DONNA. Just like that, she said she hated me. That's the way it is between parents and children. She would like me to be dead, for all she cares. I don't feel that way about her. I would like to choke her sometimes, but I wouldn't want her to be dead. Sometimes I think I would, but I really wouldn't.

STANLEY. You're both wrong. It's not about love and it's not about hate. The trouble with women is that whenever they see anything they relate it to themselves. You have to be objective.

DONNA. Objective like you? You sound exactly like Walter. I used to think you weren't like Walter. But now I see what you're like.

STANLEY. Pay attention. I'll explain it to you. It's obvious. If you weren't so hung up on your own little everyday problems you would see it clearly. The whole play, from beginning to end, is about sex. Can't you see that? It's obvious. You have

Hamlet having the hots for Ophelia. You have the uncle — what's his name? — who commits murder because he has the hots for the queen. Just look with your eyes and you'll see that's what it's about. That's what makes it so popular.

MARGARET. Stanley, I swear if I asked you what the telephone book was about, you'd say it was about sex. There's more to life than sex. In fact, if you really want to know, there's more to sex than sex.

STANLEY. Look at Walter. Why are you smirking, Walter? You think we're all ridiculous, don't you? Only *you* know the true meaning of *Hamlet*. That's what you're thinking, isn't it? High and mighty Walter. Tell us the true meaning.

WALTER. I don't know the true meaning.

STANLEY. Unbelievable. The world's leading expert on everything, and you don't know the true meaning.

WALTER. Every time I see this play, I think it means something else. I used to think it was about death. It was about accepting the fact that we're not immortal, that we're going to die sometime, and that the important thing is to choose when, and to choose the things that we feel we have to do before we die. But this performance, I saw something different. It's about betrayal. I think the whole play is about betrayal. Hamlet feels betrayed. His father *was* betrayed. Ophelia felt betrayed, and it drove her insane. Don't you see? You trust somebody completely, and then you see that that person can't be trusted. You don't believe it at first, but then you have to believe it. Maybe you think that if you love the person even more, she'll somehow become trustworthy. Like magic. But it doesn't work. Nothing works. So you learn to love without trusting. Or you stop loving. Or you lose your mind. Or you turn to sex. Or you turn to death. You embrace death. I never saw it like that before. Something happened during this performance. I think it's about betrayal.

DONNA. Betrayal. But betrayal takes two people, you know. The betrayed person is not the innocent victim. The betrayed person invites betrayal.

MARGARET. And the person who does the betraying is a victim, too. Remember that. It's no fun being a betrayer. You're betraying yourself, and you despise yourself.

STANLEY. Something's happening here. What's happening here? (*Pause.*) Look. The ushers are looking at us. We're almost the only ones here. They want us to leave. Let's go someplace and talk. Shall we go have a pizza?

WALTER. Let's get out of here. The ushers have to clean up the theater. But let's not go anywhere together. I just want to go home and talk to Donna. We have things to talk about.

MARGARET. That's a good idea. You know, Stanley, you and I have to talk, too.

STANLEY. So why can't we talk as a foursome? Like we used to?

DONNA. Because we don't want to. Do you understand?

STANLEY. So much for the four musketeers. We used to call ourselves the four musketeers.

WALTER. That's right, Stan. So much for the four musketeers.

STANLEY. Do you think the men's room is still open? I think I had too much of that Chinese wine. That plum wine. Was that what it was? I have to take another leak.

(ALL exit.)

THE END

The Old Neighborhood
DAVID MAMET

"Heart-piercing ... searing plays....[Mamet's] most
emotionally accessible drama to date."
—*The New York Times*
"This is Mamet unplugged ... a virtuoso of dialogue."
—*New York Daily News*
"Blistering, highly charged theatre."
—*Associated Press*

Bobby Gould returns to Chicago to reconnect with the people and
powerful emotions of his past. In three vignettes, he encounters an
old buddy, his sister, and a former lover. Hanging over them all is
the breakup of community, of family and the Jewish culture that
held them together. 3 m., 2 f. (#17710)

Men in Suits:
Three Plays About the Mafia
JASON MILLIGAN

"Hilarious...At turns biting, funny and sad."
—*Fairfield Country Weekly*
"Races by in an ever-changing montage of emotional
loyalty, humor, betrayal and blood.... Fascinating."
—*Connecticut Post*

Each of the three plays in this volume—*ANY FRIEND OF PERCY
D'ANGELINO IS A FRIEND OF MINE*: 2 m., 1 f. (#3577); *MEN
IN SUITS*: 3 m. (#15292); *FAMILY VALUES*: 6 m., 3 f. (#8597) —
is a riveting full-length comic drama. (#21983)

Samuel French, Inc.
SERVING THE THEATRICAL COMMUNITY SINCE 1830

Late Flowering
JOHN CHAPMAN and IAN DAVIDSON

These masters of uproarious comedy have created another delightfully funny cast of characters. Constance Beauchamp, an elegant spinster, runs a marriage bureau for the well-to-do in a fashionable area of London. She is assisted by a hard-working secretary who is set in her ways and happy with her old-fashioned filing system. Constance insists on installing a computer. The man who comes to teach them how to use it is an odd-ball bachelor who decides to feed in his own profile through the machine to find an ideal mate. After some hilarious trials and errors, Constance is alarmed to discovers it's her! 1 m., 4 f. (#13834)

The Trouble with Trent
FRED CARMICHAEL

Sparkling dialogue and laughs galore abound in this tale of mistaken identities that begins when three mystery buffs who become acquainted on the Internet E-mail chapters to each other and meet for two weeks to polish off their first book. Book sales soar when their agent hints that Sarah Trent, the pen name they use, is a real person. Meanwhile, a Washington socialite being blackmailed intends to send Sarah a story she has written about herself. She mistakenly sends the manuscript to the blackmailer and the payoff money to the three ladies behind the name Trent who have gathered to write another book. Government agents pursuing the blackmailer and a man claiming to be Mr. Trent are just two of the people who pop up. This is first-rate comedy by the popular author of numerous widely produced plays. 2 m., 6 f. (#22744)

Samuel French, Inc.
SERVING THE THEATRICAL COMMUNITY SINCE 1830

Greater Tuna
JASTON WILLIAMS, JOE SEARS and ED HOWARD

"Howlingly funny."
—*Variety*
"The audience the night I saw the show all
but exploded the theatre with laughter."
—*The New York Post*

Arles Struvie, Thurston Wheelis, Aunt Pearl and Reverend Spikes are just a few of the upstanding citizens of Tuna – Texas' third smallest town. This hilarious send-up of small-town mores involves twenty wild characters, all played by two actors in a *tour de farce* of quick-change artistry, both of costumes and characterizations. 2 m. (#9690)

A Tuna Christmas
ED HOWARD, JOE SEARS and JASTON WILLIAMS

"A hoot."
—*The New York Times*
"The hilarity never lets up."
—*The Village Voice*

It's Christmas in Tuna, Texas in this hilarious sequel to *Greater Tuna* and radio station OKKK personalities Arlis Struvie and Thurston Wheelis report on the various Yuletide activities about town. Many colorful Tuna denizens, some you will recognize from *Greater Tuna* and some appearing here for the first time, join the fun. 2 m. (#22264)

Samuel French, Inc.
SERVING THE THEATRICAL COMMUNITY SINCE 1830

Picasso at the Lapin Agile
STEVE MARTIN

"Very good fun."
NEW YORK TIMES
"Very funny ... [and] daring."
NEW YORK POST

This long-running Off-Broadway hit places Albert Einstein and Pablo Picasso in a Parisian cafe in 1904, just before the renowned scientist transformed physics and the celebrated painter set the world afire. In his first stage comedy, the popular actor and screenwriter plays fast and loose with fact, fame and fortune as these two geniuses interact with infectious dizziness. 7 m., 2 f. (#18962)

Arts & Leisure
STEVE TESICH

Written by the popular author of TOUCHING BOTTOM, ON THE OPEN ROAD, THE SPEED OF DARKNESS and other plays, this brilliantly caustic play is centered around a self-absorbed drama critic who judges theater and life by the same criteria, to absurd extremes. He is confronted by the bitter and alienated women who have suffered from his unyieldingly clinical detachment and his habit of judging their suffering by its dramatic effect on him. 1 m., 4 f. (#3866)

Samuel French, Inc.
SERVING THE THEATRICAL COMMUNITY SINCE 1830

DEATH DEFYING ACTS
David Mamet • Elaine May • Woody Allen

"An elegant diversion."
N.Y. TIMES
"A wealth of laughter."
N.Y. NEWSDAY

This Off-Broadway hit features comedies by three masters of the genre. David Mamet's brilliant twenty-minute play INTERVIEW is a mystifying interrogation of a sleazy lawyer. In HOTLINE, a wildly funny forty-minute piece by Elaine May, a woman caller on a suicide hotline overwhelms a novice counselor. A psychiatrist has discovered that her husband is unfaithful in Woody Allen's hilarious hour-long second act, CENTRAL PARK WEST. 2 m., 3 f. (#6201)

MOON OVER BUFFALO
Ken Ludwig

"Hilarious ... comic invention,
running gags {and] ... absurdity."
N.Y. POST

A theatre in Buffalo in 1953 is the setting for this hilarious backstage farce by the author of LEND ME A TENOR. Carol Burnett and Philip Bosco starred on Broadway as married thespians to whom fate gives one more shot at stardom during a madcap matinee performance of PRIVATE LIVES - or is it CYRANO DE BERGERAC? 4 m., 4 f. (#17)

Samuel French, Inc.
SERVING THE THEATRICAL COMMUNITY SINCE 1830